Life Cycles of Living Things

Reptile Life Cycle

Tracy Vonder Brink

Table of Contents

A Starfish Book

SEAHORSE PUBLISHING

Teaching Tips for Caregivers:

As a caregiver, you can help your child succeed in school by giving them a strong foundation in language and literacy skills and a desire to learn to read.

This book helps children grow by letting them practice reading skills.

Reading for pleasure and interest will help your child to develop reading skills and will give your child the opportunity to practice these skills in meaningful ways.

- Encourage your child to read on her own at home
- Encourage your child to practice reading aloud
- Encourage activities that require reading
- Establish a reading time
- Talk with your child
- Give your child writing materials

Teaching Tips for Teachers:

Research shows that one of the best ways for students to learn a new topic is to read about it.

Before Reading

- Read the "Words to Know" and discuss the meaning of each word.
- Read the back cover to see what the book is about.

During Reading

- When a student gets to a word that is unknown, ask them to look at the rest of the sentence to find clues to help with the meaning of the unknown word.
- Ask the student to write down any pages of the book that were confusing to them.

After Reading

- Discuss the main idea of the book.
- Ask students to give one detail that they learned in the book by showing a text dependent answer from the book.

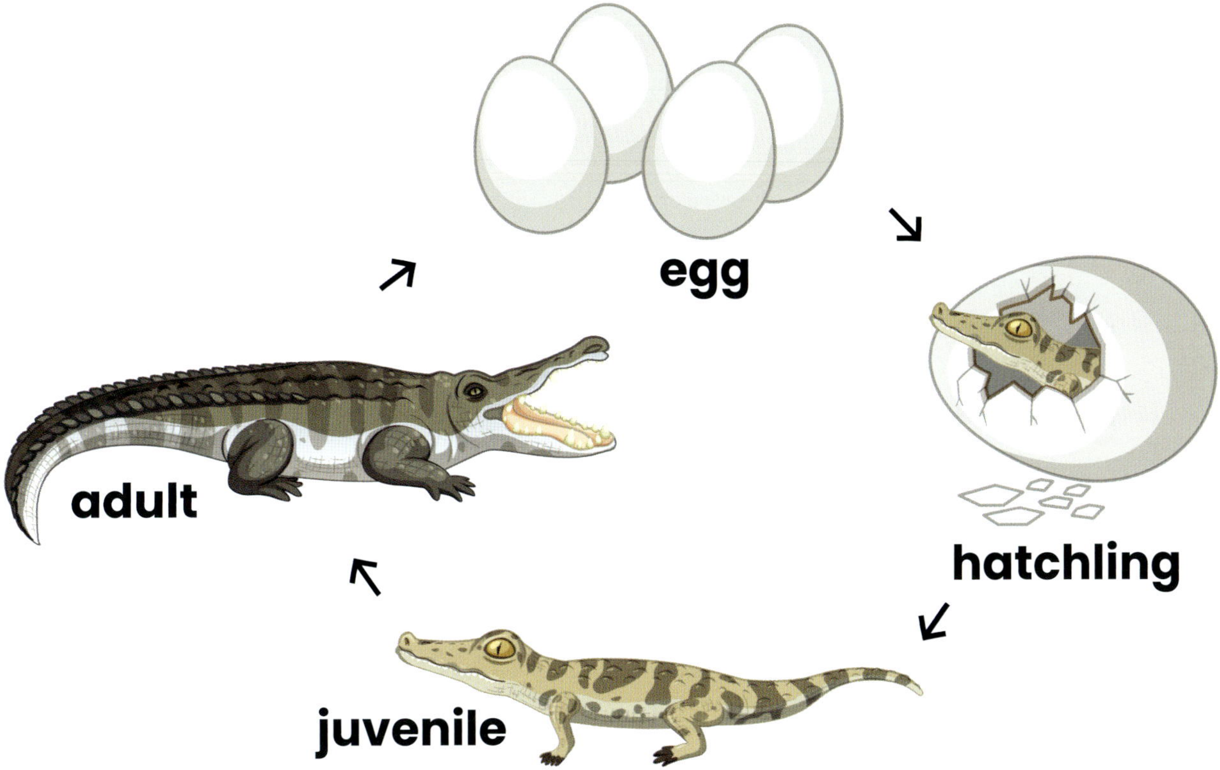

Reptile Life Cycle

All living things are born.

They grow to be adults.

We call these changes a life cycle.

Reptiles are animals with backbones.

Their bodies are covered in **scales**.

Reptiles are **cold-blooded**.

Reptiles use lungs to breathe air.

A reptile's life cycle begins with an egg.

The egg has a soft shell.

An **embryo** grows inside.

A group of eggs is called a clutch.

The embryo becomes a **hatchling**.

The hatchling breaks out of the egg.

It has the same **features** as an adult reptile.

Most reptile hatchlings live on their own.

No parent cares for them.

The hatchling finds its own food.

It grows into a **juvenile**.

Many reptiles eat insects.
Some also eat plants.

The juvenile looks like a grown reptile.

But it cannot yet have its own babies.

The juvenile becomes an adult.

The adult reptile is ready to find a mate.

Most reptiles find mates in the spring.

Some male reptiles show bright colors to attract females.

The females choose the most colorful males.

The females lay eggs.

The life cycle begins again.

Words to Know

cold-blooded (kohld BLUHD-id): unable to make body heat; having a body temperature that changes with the temperature of the surroundings

embryo (EM-bree-oh): a living creature in the earliest stage of development, before it is hatched or born

features (FEE-churz): parts, qualities, or characteristics; the features of an animal's body include its legs, tail, eyes, etc.

hatchling (HACH-ling): a young animal that has newly hatched from an egg

juvenile (JOO-vuh-nile): a young living creature that has not yet reached its adult form

scales (skales): small, flat, thin plates that cover the bodies of some animals, such as reptiles

Index

Comprehension Questions

1. A reptile's life cycle begins with
a. a hatchling. **b.** a juvenile. **c.** an egg.

2. Most reptile hatchlings live
a. with a parent.
b. on their own.
c. with a group of hatchlings.

3. Some male reptiles attract female reptiles by
a. showing bright colors.
b. croaking the loudest.
c. running the fastest.

4. **True or false:** Hatchling reptiles find their own food.

5. **True or false:** Juvenile reptiles are able to have babies.

Answers
1. c 2. b 3. a 4. True 5. False

About the Author

Tracy Vonder Brink loves true stories and facts. She has written more than twenty books for kids and is a contributing editor for three children's science magazines. Tracy lives in Cincinnati, Ohio, with her husband, two daughters, and two rescue dogs.

Written by: Tracy Vonder Brink
Design by: Bobbie Houser
Editor: Kim Thompson

Library of Congress PCN Data
Reptile Life Cycle / Tracy Vonder Brink
Life Cycles of Living Things
ISBN 978-1-63897-456-7 (hard cover)
ISBN 978-1-63897-571-7 (paperback)
ISBN 978-1-63897-686-8 (EPUB)
ISBN 978-1-63897-801-5 (eBook)
Library of Congress Control Number: 2021953364

Printed in the United States of America.

Photographs:
t = Top, b = Bottom, c = Center, l = Left, r = Right

Shutterstock: Chatchawal Kittirojana: cover tl; Catchlight Lens: cover tr; Ondrej Prosicky: cover b; BlueRingMedia: p. 3; Kurit afshen: p. 5 t; Shadska Photo: p. 5 b; COULANGES: p. 7; WeStudio: p. 8; Kevin Wells Photography: pp. 10-11; davemhuntphotography: p. 13; Rob Yoder: p. 14; Fercast: p. 17; Hemant Arun Chhatre: pp. 18-19; Jirapong nontakanan: p. 20

Seahorse Publishing Company
www.seahorsepub.com

Published in the United States
Seahorse Publishing
PO Box 771325
Coral Springs, FL 33077

SEAHORSE PUBLISHING